SMALL GREAT GESTURES

SCIENCE

Francisco Llorca

Illustrated by

Iker Ayestaran

Translated by Emma Martinez

'It wouldn't be much of a universe
if it wasn't home to the people you love.'
STEPHEN HAWKING

SMALL GREAT GESTURES
SCIENCE

Science is not just a collection of facts about different subjects, it is also a way to get to know and understand the world we live in. There have been many curious minds throughout history that have tried to understand the laws of nature, posing questions and persevering until they found the answers. Thanks to them, we have succeeded in travelling into space, we exchange information on the internet and have found cures for diseases that we once thought could never be cured.

This book collects some of the moments of extraordinary and sudden illumination that have changed our lives and made our world a little bit bigger.

Nevertheless, what is still unexplored is immense, ranging from the tiniest particles to the boundaries of the known universe. Years ago, we knew nothing about the structure of DNA or the infinite possibilities of the internet. We cannot predict what will happen in the next few years, but we know that curious minds and indomitable spirits are already among us. And who knows, maybe you will be one of them ...

FRANCISCO LLORCA

Eat an Apple
SIR ISAAC NEWTON

England, 1666

One evening, Isaac Newton was strolling around his garden when he saw an apple fall from a tree. Of course, this was nothing unusual, all fruit falls when it is ripe. But it stirred young Newton's curiosity and he asked himself how the apple came to fall, when the moon in the night sky did not?

The answer to this question is gravity; an invisible force that attracts objects towards one another. The same force that attracted the apple towards the ground also attracts the moon. But the moon doesn't fall to earth because its orbit around our planet counteracts the force of gravity (just like when two people of the same strength pull on the ends of a rope). The same forces keep the earth and the planets spinning around the sun. Beginning with the falling apple story, Newton was able to explain the laws that govern the movements of the planets.

Whenever you eat an apple, remember the story of this English scientist whose discoveries illuminated a new way of viewing the universe.

Observe Nature
CHARLES DARWIN

Ecuador, 1835

Charles Darwin was a restless and curious young man. He could spend hours on end observing and drawing plants and birds. So, when he was encouraged to sign up for a place on the *Beagle*, a ship about to set sail around the world, he did not hesitate.

During the voyage, Darwin was able to study the plants and animals of other continents. It was on the Galapagos Islands off the coast of Ecuador that he observed small differences in the same species of bird, depending on which island he visited. On one island the bird had a shorter beak, on another it was curved, and on the farthest islands, the beak was narrower ... This observation seemed small and unimportant, but over time it helped him formulate his theory of evolution that would change the way we understand how life appeared and developed on earth.

The young naturalist discovered that those bird species shared a common ancestor but had adapted over time to their different environments through a process called 'natural selection'. When Darwin returned home five years later, he explained how humans are also subject to this process and that we therefore share our ancestry with other animals, like monkeys. But this caused a scandal that divided society in his day. Today, thanks to his observations, humans are able to recognise their place in the scheme of life.

V_0

$+$
0
0
0
0

Programme

ADA LOVELACE

England, 1843

Ada Lovelace was an intelligent and brave visionary who lived her life against the grain. In her time, women were considered to be their husband's property and their place to be in the home. But it was clear from the beginning that Ada, daughter of a famous women's rights activist and a famous poet, would not follow that path.

When she was very young, she began collaborating with Charles Babbage, the inventor of the Analytical Engine, which was like an enormous calculator and a was a distant relative of today's computers. Ada saw a world of possibilities in the machine far beyond number crunching, and anticipated the future age of computing. For Ada, these machines would become extensions of human thought and help us to do almost anything (for example, she was convinced they could be used to compose music). Today, over two centuries later, we know she was right.

Ada dedicated herself to explaining the complex workings of this invention, using a sophisticated system of pierced cards to operate it and store data. Today, her instructions and cards are considered to have been the first ever computer programme.

m'

.....
.....
.....
....

0

.....
.....
....

.....

Number of Operations	Name of Operations	$^i V_1$
		$+$
		0
		0
		0
		1
		m
1	χ	n
2	χ	.....
3	χ	.....
4	χ	.....
5	χ	0
6	χ	......
7	χ	.....
8	χ	......
9	χ	.....
10	χ	......
11	χ	......

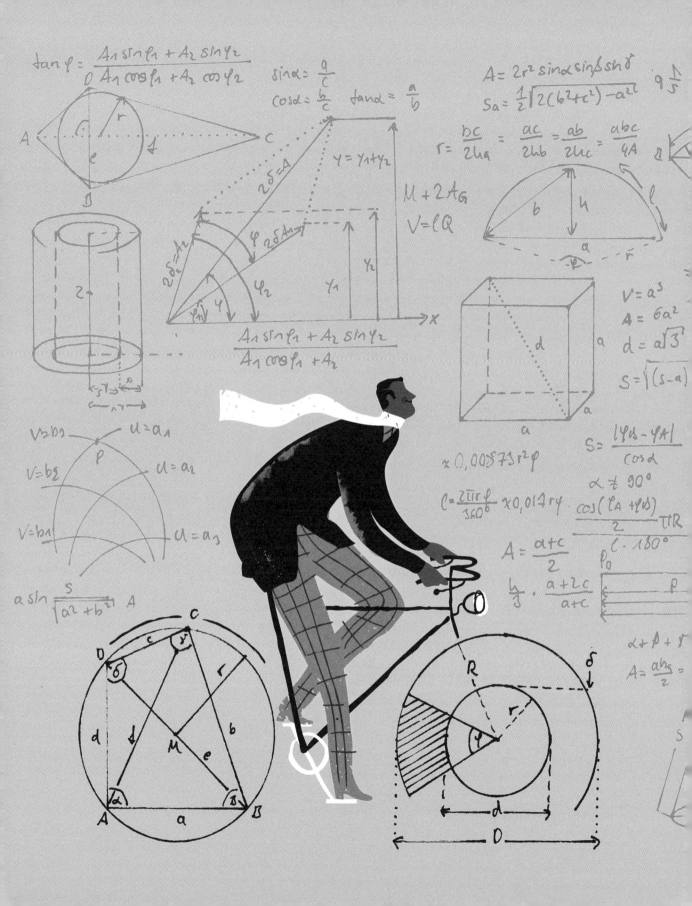

SRINIVASA RAMANUJAN

India, 1913

Ramanujan lived with his parents in a small Indian city, when at the age of eleven he discovered mathematics in a schoolbook. The discovery changed his life for ever. As though he was playing a game, Ramanujan jotted down his ideas and formulas in notebooks that amazed his teachers and school friends. These games and formulas ended up in the hands of a prestigious mathematician, Harold Hardy, who noticed that the young man saw formulas and structures in numbers that other humans were incapable of seeing.

Hardy realised Ramanujan was a self-taught genius and invited him to visit England, paying for the trip himself. Hardy became his mentor and collaborator at Cambridge University, one of the most important universities in the world.

In those days, the university was a very conservative place. Many of Ramanujan's companions didn't accept him because of where he came from, and because he had no classical training. Nevertheless, his intellect was far beyond theirs, and he made extraordinary contributions towards the analysis of mathematics. He published a vast number of articles that to this day continue to amaze the world with their brilliance and intelligence.

Travel

MARGARET MEAD

New Guinea, 1931

Travelling not only allows you to get to know new places, but also the people who live there and how they live. Sometimes, this may be very different to how you live, which makes you ask questions. The American, Margaret Mead, dedicated most of her life to asking questions and looking for answers.

Margaret travelled constantly throughout Southeast Asia, studying the habits of different native communities and noticed lots of differences between the roles of men and women in each of them. For instance, in some societies women went to work and took care of the practical side of things, while the men stayed at home. This showed that the roles of men and women in society were not determined by nature, but by society itself, and that therefore they could be changed. Women do not necessarily have to take care of the home or the family, as was believed by American society (and many others).

Margaret's studies contributed towards the questioning of a whole series of prejudices and stereotypes, laying the ground for the principles of gender equality.

Embrace Accidents
ALEXANDER FLEMING

England, 1928

In many of the greatest human discoveries, chance, luck and coincidence have played an essential role. Even making mistakes has led to important discoveries. All of these things played a part with Alexander Fleming.

Fleming served as a doctor in France during the First World War. The death of thousands of young people due to wounds that became infected made a big impression on him and he decided to dedicate the rest of his life to finding possible remedies to this problem.

Fleming worked hard to find a possible solution and had some good results. However, his greatest discovery came in 1928, when he returned to his laboratory after being on holiday for a few days. He discovered that he had accidentally contaminated one of his experiments, which meant a fungus had grown and destroyed the bacteria he had been studying (bacteria are the microorganisms that cause lots of diseases). He managed to extract penicillin from this fungus, an antibiotic that fights infections caused by bacteria. And so, although accidentally, his mistake saved millions of lives.

Fleming did not patent his discovery, which meant that the whole world could benefit from it. In 1945 he was awarded the Nobel Prize in Medicine in recognition of his determination and generosity.

Dissolve
GEORGE DE HEVESY

Denmark, 1940

The Nobel Prize is the most important award given each year to people who have researched or made outstanding contributions towards human development. In recognition of the winners, the organisation hands out gold medals with the winners' names engraved on them.

George de Hevesy was a well-known chemist who had to hide three of these medals in his laboratory during the Second World War. The interesting thing is that none of these medals were his. They belonged to other scientists who gave them to Hevesy to hide so that the Germans would not seize them, because the winners were Jewish or anti-Nazis. In order to hide them, Hevesy devised a plan that left no trace. He decided to dissolve them in a substance (like cubes of sugar in hot tea). When the Nazi soldiers searched the laboratory, they could not find any medals, even though they were right in front of their noses.

At the end of the war, Hevesy recovered the gold using a chemical process and gave it back to the Nobel Prize organisers, who minted the medals again and returned them to their rightful owners.

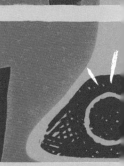

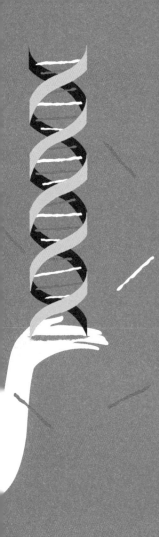

Take a Photo
ROSALIND FRANKLIN

England, 1952

Just like in other fields, women in science do not enjoy the same opportunities as men. The most important and best-paid jobs are usually given to men. This is unfair, as many of the essential discoveries in the advancement of humanity were made by women. One such case is that of Rosalind Franklin.

As a child, Rosalind decided to dedicate her life to science. She was a brilliant student, and when she finished her studies she left for France, where she learned the photographic technique that would enable her discovery of the true structure of DNA.

DNA is the molecule that contains all of our genetic information, like the information on your passport. To put it another way, DNA is to life what letters are to books: small pieces that, when placed one way or another, say different things.

But in those days it was hard to be a female scientist – Rosalind was not allowed into the professors' lounge just because she was a woman. Her work was undervalued by institutions, and her photos and discoveries were used by other male scientists without her permission. Thanks to her work, the men who used her photos won the Nobel Prize. The crucial role that Rosalind had played was only discovered later.

Take a Leap
VALENTINA TERECHKOVA

Soviet Union, 1963

From her humble origins, nothing suggested that Valentina would end up becoming the first woman to travel to space. Born in a remote village in Russia, her father was a tractor driver and her mother worked in a textile factory. Valentina also worked in a textile factory while completing her education through correspondence courses. In her spare time, she would practise her favourite hobby: parachute jumping.

Inspired by the adventures of her compatriot, Yuri Gagarin (the first human to travel into space) and encouraged by her love of heights, Valentina auditioned for a new space adventure, and was selected out of over four hundred candidates because of her daring and dedication. This was how, after joining the Cosmonaut Programme in 1963, she took the biggest leap of her life, spending three days in orbit and completing over forty-eight trips around the earth.

When she was more than sixty years old, she was the torchbearer for the Winter Olympic Games held in her country. She still dreams of returning to space.

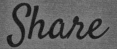

Share
RICHARD STALLMAN

United States of America, 1982

A computer is made up of many different components; the parts you can touch (keyboard, mouse, screen...) and a series of programmes that enable you to work or play. These programmes you can't touch are called the software.

There are two types of software: those that allow users to control the programme, and those that control users through a series of restrictions (these are usually paid programmes and cannot be shared or copied). Richard Stallman dedicated most of his life to developing software that is free , can be modified by users and shared with others.

In 1982 he created GNU, a free operating system. With this software, Stallman favoured individual choice and the ability to do what you want with the programme. He encouraged collaboration among users, creating a community of helpful people that aimed to share information and in turn, to help others in society.

Research
FRANÇOISE BARRÉ-SINOUSSI

France, 1983

At the start of the 1980s, doctors began seeing cases of a strange illness that ended the lives of many people in a very short time. The race was on to find a cure for the disease called Acquired Immune Deficiency Syndrome, known as AIDS.

Doctor Françoise Barré-Sinoussi played a crucial role in this race, since it was her research that helped identify the virus and offer treatment that, although it did not cure the disease, reduced its effects and allowed the people who had it to live longer.

Françoise received the 2008 Nobel prize in Medicine along with her colleague, Luc Montagnier, for their discoveries, but she knew that education was just as important as science in the fight against this disease. Which is why, while continuing to seek a cure for the illness, she shares information on the virus and how to protect against it with the whole world, particularly in developing countries.

Never Give Up
STEPHEN HAWKING

England, 2018

Stephen Hawking was a brilliant young scientist who wanted to explain the origins of the universe, when a terrible illness left him largely paralysed. He was forced to use a wheelchair to get around, and had to communicate through a computer.

Despite his illness, Stephen continued to question the theories of space and time, determined to find answers. His research opened up a world of possibilities to science and his tireless work as a teacher and through books, documentaries and conferences, brought the stars closer to millions of people.

But beyond his scientific discoveries, his greatest contribution was to show people that you can follow your dreams no matter what. His triumph over adversity inspired millions of people around the world and he became proof of the infinite possibilities of the human mind.

Eat an Apple
Sir Isaac Newton
England, 1666

Observe Nature
Charles Darwin
Ecuador, 1835

Programme
Ada Lovelace
England, 1843

Play
Srinivasa Ramanujan
India, 1913

Travel
Margaret Mead
New Guinea, 1931

Embrace Accidents
Alexander Fleming
England, 1928

Dissolve
George de Hevesy
Denmark, 1940

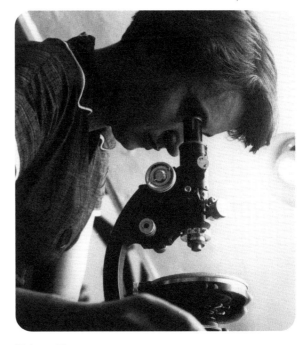

Take a Photo
Rosalind Franklin
England, 1952

Take a Leap
Valentina Tereshkova
Soviet Union, 1963

Share
Richard Stallman
United States of America, 1982

Research
Françoise Barré-Sinoussi
France, 1983

Never Give Up
Stephen Hawking
England, 2018

© Francisco Llorca, 2018
© Ilustrations: Iker Ayestaran, 2018
Graphic Design: Pepe & James; Christina Griffiths

Photographic acknowledgements

Portrait of Isaac Newton © Godfrey Kneller [Public domain] / Wikimedia Commons

Charles Darwin (1809-1882) in his last years © J. Cameron / Wikimedia Commons

(Augusta) Ada King, Countess Lovelace (1815-1852) Matematician, daughter of Lord Byron © Margaret Sarah Carpenter (1793-1872) / Wikimedia Commons

Srinivasa Ramanujan © Unknown author / Wikimedia Commons

Margaret Mead on her travels © Tomste1808, under licence of Creative Commons / Wikimedia Commons

Professor Alexander Fleming in his laboratory at St Mary's, Paddington (London) © Official Photographer of the Imperial War Museum / IWM Media

George de Hevesy (1913) / Wikimedia Commons

Rosalind Franklin with her microscope © Henry Grant Archive

Valentina Tereshkova, pictured as a Major of the Soviet Air Forces © Alexander Mokletsov / RIA Novosti Archive

Richard Stallman / Image courtesy of stallman.org

Françoise Barré-Sinoussi at a press conference at the Karolinska Institute (Solna) © GNU Free Documentation License

Stephen Hawking © Topham / Cordon Press

First published in Spain in 2018 under the title *Pequeños grandes gestos por la ciencia*
by Alba Editorial, s.l.u.
Baixada de Sant Miquel, 1, 08002 Barcelona
albaeditorial.es

First published in the UK in 2021 by Allison and Busby
11 Wardour Mews
London W1F 8AN
allisonandbusby.com

A CIP catalogue record for this book is available from
the British Library.

ISBN 978-0-7490-2703-2

MIX
Paper from
responsible sources
FSC® C118234
FSC
www.fsc.org

Also available

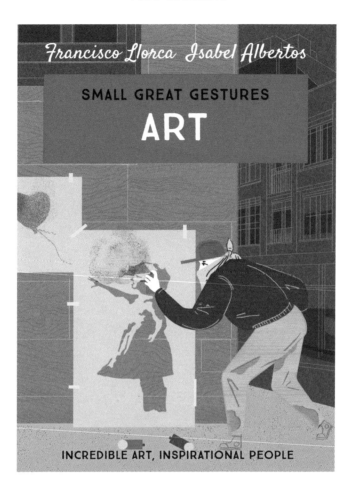

From the Renaissance to the present day, this inspiring book paints a vivid picture of the lives and works of eleven artists who stood out from the crowd and changed how we see the world.

Beginning with Giotto in Florence and ending with Banksy's international street art, and including Picasso in the Spanish Civil War and Frida Kahlo in 1920s Mexico, *Art* is a beautiful and entertaining book for budding artists everywhere.